Wakefield Press

CORNISH PASTY

Cornish Pasty

A selection of cartoons

Oswald Pryor

Wakefield Press

Wakefield Press
16 Rose Street
Mile End
South Australia 5031
www.wakefieldpress.com.au

First published by Rigby Limited as *Cornish Pasty* copyright © Oswald Pryor
1961 and *Cousin Jacks and Jennys* copyright © Oswald Pryor 1966
Published in combination with Seal Books 1976

This edition published 2025

Copyright © Oswald Pryor, 1961, 1966, 1976, 2025

All rights reserved. This book is copyright. Apart from any fair dealing for the
purposes of private study, research, criticism or review, as permitted under
the Copyright Act, no part may be reproduced without written permission.
Enquiries should be addressed to the publisher.

Scanned and redesigned by Wakefield Press

ISBN 978 1 92338 812 3

 A catalogue record for this book is available from the National Library of Australia

 Wakefield Press thanks Coriole Vineyards for continued support

THE FIRST MOONTA MINER

Copper was first discovered at Moonta in 1861, at the mound of a wombat.

The wombat was followed by hundreds of other miners, from Cornwall.

"It was the general belief of the Tres, Pols, and Pens who descended on the Moonta district about 100 years ago that they had gone there to mine copper and being conscientious fellows, mine copper they did, oblivious of the fact that their real function in life was to provide raw material for the cartoons of Oswald Pryor."

—W. E. Fitzhenry
in *The Bulletin*

"Wha's up? Horse is down, tha's wha's up!"

"Near nuff won't do, got to be zact."
"Tez zact."
"Well, tha's near nuff."

"Gosh, Cap'n got un in the neck that time!"

"I've tried everything and I can't get it to go."
"Tried pushin', av un, Maister?"

"Psst! Ask my missus if it's time to put the pasties in th' oven?"

"Dussent bump into me, I'm takin' 'ome the width of a door."

"That danged shoemaker! I told un to make one boot longer than t'other and 'e went and made one shorter than t'other."

"'T would'n s'prise me Nick'las, if you lasted 'nuther couple o' weeks."

"'Ow did'ee enjoy your trip 'ome to Cornwall, Maister Treeloar?"
"Splendid, John; I sing'd to fower funerals."

"Seven's too many; haff of 'ee come up."

"That maid d' play organ accordin' to scripture—'Let not the right hand know what the left doeth'."

"I thought it was Billy Bilcock goin' up, an' 'e thought 't was me comin' deown, but when we met 't wadden neither one of us."

"Listen to our departed brother's dying words, 'Bury me in me old red guernsey'."
"Allellooyer! 'E won't want no guernsey where 'e's gone to."

"Damn 'ee, I've taught 'ee all I knaw, and neow theece dunnaw nuthin'."

"Lend me your axe, boay; I d' want to saw a piece of timber to put up a fowl 'ouse to kape a pig in."

"Bisect that stull piece into three equal parts."

"'Ow did your doctor-son get on with his first confinement?"
"Splendid, Cap'n. Mother and cheel died, but 'e saved the feyther."

"Can't understand 'ow I got the sack, boay, I burnt twice s'much coal as they other stokers."

"Ole man Trebuzza's been and dropped dead on 'is ninety-fourth birthday."
"Baint surprised. 'E was always delicate."

"One an' a haff, plaze."

"If all 'is brains was ink, boay, 'e wouldn' 'ave enough to write a full stop."

"Who be they toffs?"
"Mind your work, boay; they be the Board of Disciples."

"Beats me 'ow they all knawed I coomed from Moonta."

"What do you think of ole man's new patent wheelbarrow, Mister?"
"Wha's new 'bout un, m'son?"
"'Andles in front and wheel behind."

"When I say a thing is, it IS, even if 'tedden."

"Next item on program is Chairman's Address. If any of 'ee don't knaw, tez twenty-nine Fried-tatey Street."

"Haff-minute, Lizbeth, we're a-movin' the pianner."

"Only one-and-six tribute, Cap'n? Why, that edden nuthin'."
"Better take un, boays; nuthin's better than nuthin' 't all."

"Why, Mawther, you d' look like one o' they glammer girls."

"During lighting restrictions, evenin' service will be 'eld in the afternoon."

"Neow, mind, if I give 'ee a trial, you must pull your weight."

"Had any experience with explosives?"
"Exper'unce, Cap'n! I've been blawed to bits three times."

"'Ow 're 'ee gettin' on, boay?"

"'E's been preachin' fifty year, Tummas."
"'Bout time 'e stopped, I'm feeling 'ungry."

"Where be goin'?"
"Baint goin' nowhere; been where I'm goin'."

"Stop 'ollerin', brother, the Looard edden deaf."

"'E guv'd one chance, Cap'n, but lucky for un there wadden nobody there to take it."

New Parson: "Goodbye, Mr. Tredisseck, and may the better side win, I say."
Cousin Jack: "Same 'ere, m'son; and it will, too, if us can get they other chaps out 'fore they score too many runs."

"We'll be wantin' seats in the aisles, Mister Tresize, Cap'n 'Ancock ez takin' the service."

"My dotter will now sing, 'Alice Where Be Gone To'."

"Why don't you buy a trumpet, Trebuzza?"
"Cudden play un, if I did."

"C'mon, boays; double f's, guv-un-guts."

"Dear, dear! Some people do show their ignorance. Why, it's the 'Lost Chord' from 'The Messiah'."

"Never 'eard tell o' Moscow, laad? Why, that's where old Boneyparty met his Waterloo."

"'S all 'is own fault, doctor; 'e will keep tryin' to say them Russian war names."

"Looard, we'm all gone rusty and do want ilin (oiling).
Pour out thine ile 'pon us—the ile of Patmos."

"My father came from Penzance, I believe?"
"Tha's right; I knawed all the fam'ly. Your granfather were 'ung."

"Ever been up in one, laad?"

"Countin' eighty to the pound, Cap'n there was nigh 'pon fower 'undred in chapel 's' mornin'."

"Gosh! Is that only one woman?"

"Did 'ee ever see two more alike than Silas and John, 'n' speshully John?"

"Only me an' God'll ever know who I voted for, Maister, and 'E would'n know if I could 'elp it."

"Ez it true you've resigned, Cap'n?"
"Iss, m'son, I'm only a common man, now."

"Fetch the saw, boay; this piece is too long one end."

"If I d' live till mornin', and all's well, I'll stop in bed sick with the doctor."

"The sack doant worry me, boay. I got enough to live on, if I died tomorrow."

"Let un up, boay, let un up! 'E 've 'ad 'nough."
"Shan't let un up, too damn 'ard to git un deown."

"What say, boays? Shall us 'ave a drop o' beer an' praise one another up a bit?"

"Ssh! Caan't 'ee see I be talkin' to Cap'n 'Ancock?"

Bride's Father (to groom who is finding the ring tight):
"Suck 'er finger, boay!"

"Never spent a penny on frivolity all the time I was away, 'cept a shillun to 'ear 'The Messiah'."

"Goo' night, Cap'n."

"Welcome to our footballers! My text is from Matthew VIII:32—'Into the swine'."

"Capital! What IS Capital?"
"If you was to ask we to come 'n' 'ave a drink, lad, that would be capital."

"I called Cap'n 'Ancock all the rotters in the world but I said it to meself."

"Which one of you twins is home in bed with measles, dear?"

"Lor', I wouldn't like to go down with a little rope like that!"
"Be worse without un, Missus."

"Accidents! I've had three legs broke, now."

"My ol' man drank all his life, 'n' if he was livin' he'd be a hundred."

"Gunpowder, Cap'n! There ain't a man had more experience widdun."

"That's not a note, that's a fly."
"Can't help it. I played 'n."

"Notice anything about the car—anything at all?"
"Iss! 'E were a fower-wheeler."

"Look! Cap'n's out 'oss-riding' 's mornin'."

"Met a lot of old friends up township, I'd never seen before, 'n' 'ad a couple too many."

"The remarkable part, Missus, is the way they meet dead in the middle."

"What'd make that needle always point north, Cap'n?"
"Think I'm goin' tell you in five minutes what took me years to find out?"

When Father Does A Job.

"'Ow many enemy 'planes 'ave 'ee brought down, lad?"

"'Ardly like to tell 'ee, Cap'n, but they alterations is a bad improvement."

"That furriner chap, Cap'n, d'speak Hinglish purty near as good as me 'n' you."

"Bain't burr'd a livin' soul for six months, Cap'n."

"Tur-r-nips, penny each! Too busy to stop, Missus!"

"What steps would you take if steam pressure went up to two hundred pounds?"
"Longest ones I could, Cap'n."

"Fifty-two weeks in the year 'n' you must pick Show Week to look for that squeak."

"Mine's the one white washed yeller."

"Chap what made that, Tummus, didn' knaw much 'bout a locomotive!"

"Wake up, Tummus, time t' swaller your sleepin'-draught."

"'Tedden all beer 'n' skittles bein' a parson, Maister?"

"Where 'e's marked 'con fuoco', boays, tha's Latin for guv un guts."

"Just the man! Jump up boay, the horn's gone bung."

"Inflation! Wan time y' could git a fivepenny stamp for tuppence."

"— now turn to the Prodigal Son; slouching along, hands in pockets, seat of his pants out, and mother home making a pasty for him."

"Two thirds of 'em on this mine don't know the way in out of a shower of rain."

"If y' call THIS religion, I'm done widdun."

"Hullo, there! Put me on to wha's-'is-name."

"As for Missus, Cap'n, she's a lady, FIT for any comp'ny."

"This place edden fit for a man to go into, Cap'n. Come in and have a look at un."

"Hear that? 'In my Father's house are many mansions.'
His father's house is a little ol' scrub hut."

"Loard, save the people! You don't know 'aff what's going on down here, Loard."

"Let some drops now fall on me."

"Oo made your nice suit, deear?"
"Nobody. Bought made 'n' all."

"Know any croonin' pieces, boay?"
"Only 'Croon Un Lord of All'."

"Mawther! Kettle's boilin' over."

"Hey! Where's Cap'n?"

"Caan't read it, boay, but if I had me trombone I'd play it for 'ee."

"I always prefer long-'andle shovel, Cap'n—better for leanin' on."

"Our tennis club was top, our cricketers made the highest aggregate score, our gymnasium is growing and our young people's club spent many happy evenings."
"Uss! And 'ow many souls did 'ee save from 'ternal fire 'n' brimstone?"

"St Paul wrote a passel of letters, my friends, but he didn't have to pay five pence postage on them."

"I bain't Coornish, Missus, but feyther an' mawther was."

"I would rather be a doorkeeper in the House of the Lord, than a chucker-out in a circus tent."

"I would like to assure our departin' guests that this is the most pop'lar sendoff we ever guv anybody."

"Wha's 'ee got there, boay; Broken 'ill racehorse?"

"Word has come that Cap'n Trebuzza is dead. Let us rise and sing, 'Praise God from Whom All Blessings Flow'."

"'Aff the time, doc, I don't know whether I'm on me 'ead or me 'eels."

"*Must be gettin' tottery, Tummas—got stull-piece under un.*"

"Look, boay! Automation!"

"From Broken 'ill, lad? An' what chapel did 'ee b'long up there?"

"Lizbeth Jane's solo was lovely. Oo do she git 'er voice from?"
"From Granfer, of coorse. 'E used to play bass viol in Camborne choir."

"Once you sign this pledge, lad, you mustn't drink, smoke, bet, lie, steal, swear—."
"Can I spit, Mister?"

"Far East, Tummas? 'E's up nor'-west."

"Is it a powerful organ, Mr Trepolpen?"
"Powerful? First time they played un' 'e blawed out all the windows."

Wakefield Press is an independent publishing and
distribution company based in Adelaide, South Australia.
We love good stories and publish beautiful books.
To see our full range of books, please visit our website at
www.wakefieldpress.com.au
where all titles are available for purchase.
To keep up with our latest releases, news and events,
subscribe to our monthly newsletter.

Find us!

Facebook: www.facebook.com/wakefield.press
Instagram: www.instagram.com/wakefieldpress

www.ingramcontent.com/pod-product-compliance
Lightning Source LLC
Chambersburg PA
CBHW032301150426
43195CB00008BA/537